LAD NN

L

FERRY Publications

PO BOX 33, RAMSEY, ISLE OF MAN, IM99 4LP TEL: +44 (0) 1624 898446 FAX: +44 (0) 1624 898449

ISBN 1 871947 69 3

(Rick Tomlinson)

(Second Edition 2001)

FOREWORD

It gives me great pleasure to write the foreword to this book by John Shepherd about our fine vessel the *Lady of Mann*.

Already, the 'Lady' has had a long, varied and interesting career, but there is a way to go yet. Modified in 2001 to meet the latest SOLAS and Stockholm Agreement requirements, she remains a key part of the Steam Packet fleet.

The 'Lady' is a well-loved vessel, still popular 25 years after her introduction to service. The Irish Sea is a testing arena for ships, but throughout many a gale the 'Lady' has proved up to the job. Her record of reliability is a proud one.

Joining the Steam Packet in 1992, I always thought of the 'Lady' as 'Vernon's' ship. Throughout many years, Captain Vernon Kinley was associated with the 'Lady' as her Master. His death in 1998 was a sad loss to so many. This book, which I am sure will be a great read for many ship lovers everywhere, will also serve to remind us of a very fine Shipmaster.

Hamish Ross

Managing Director, Isle of Man Steam Packet Co. Ltd

Hamish Ross

INTRODUCTION

The *Lady of Mann* was built by the Ailsa Shipbuilding Company Limited (Yard No 547) at Troon, Ayrshire, and was launched on 4th December 1975. The new 'Lady' was the sixty-third vessel to be owned and operated by the Isle of Man Steam Packet Company in its long history going back to 1830. The Company's policy over the years had been to purpose-build its own vessels and forty-seven of the fleet had been constructed to its own specifications, only sixteen having been brought in 'second-hand', mainly in the 1920s following the First World War. However the new *Lady of Mann* proved to be the last of the line as far as purpose-built ships were concerned: in the 1980s shipping patterns were changing rapidly with the roll on-roll off revolution, and the Steam Packet's introduction of SeaCat services in 1994 led to the 'Lady' becoming effectively redundant, although she was 'good' for at least another ten years. Shipbuilding costs were also spiralling throughout the 1980s to the point where the Company could not afford to build its own ships; for instance the 'Lady' cost £3.8 million, whereas just eight years later, in 1984, the lowest tender for a multi-purpose ro-ro vessel exceeded £20 million.

THE NEW 'LADY' ENTERS SERVICE

In spite of all the pressure brought to bear and the efforts made by the Ailsa Shipbuilding Company, the *Lady of Mann* was not delivered in time to cope with the peak traffic at the time of the TT Races in early June 1976, which put tremendous pressure on the remaining six units of the fleet. The matter of late delivery was taken up with Ailsa who were also very distressed by their failure to effect delivery on the due date. It must be appreciated that a shipyard depends to a large extent on components manufactured by other

The magnificent ***Lady of Mann*** (I) arriving at Douglas in July 1970. *(Paul Clegg)*

companies and on specialised work carried out by sub-contractors, and it is clear that Ailsa were badly let down in some of these respects.

The *Lady of Mann* successfully completed her trials on 24th June, and the Isle of Man Steam Packet Company took delivery six days later. The 'Lady's' maiden arrival at Douglas was at 20.35 on 29th June. On a still, sunny summer evening the new vessel slipped into her berth on the North Edward pier. Her sister, the *Mona's Queen* of 1972, lay on the South Edward. The new vessel's maiden voyage was from Douglas to Liverpool at 09.00 on 30th June and on arrival in the Mersey she was given the traditional welcome by the *Mona's Isle* [5].

It quickly became apparent that the new *Lady of Mann* was a faster ship than the *Mona's Queen*. Her twin 12 cylinder main engines (as against the 10 cylinder engines of the 'Queen') could produce more than 11,500 horsepower at 465 rpm, giving a maximum speed of almost 23 knots if required. The 'Lady' did not suffer the early vibration problems of her older sister.

THE FIRST LADY

The *Lady of Mann* was the second holder of the name in the Steam Packet fleet. The first 'Lady' was built at Vickers, Armstrong Limited at Barrow in Furness in 1930 and was launched on 4th March. She made her maiden voyage from Fleetwood to Douglas on 28th June 1930 and at 3,104 gross tons was, until the arrival of the present *Ben-my-Chree,* the largest vessel ever built for the Steam Packet Company. The *Lady of Mann* [1] cost £249,073 to build, had a speed of 22.5 knots and in pre-war years boasted a passenger certificate for as many as 2,873.

During the Second World War the 'Lady' was present at Dunkerque and brought out 4,262 troops on four round trips. At the D-Day landings she was a Landing Ship (Infantry) carrying six landing assault craft and was Headquarters ship for the 512th Assault Flotilla at Juno Beach near Corseulles-sur-Mer.

The *Lady of Mann* [1] returned to Douglas on 9th March 1946 and after being refitted by Cammell Laird, she sailed every summer until 1971. She could be recognised in fog by her triple chime whistle which had a particularly deep and melodious tone. The old 'Lady' left Douglas for the last time on 17th August 1971 and received an emotional 'Farewell' from several thousand people lining the piers and promenade. After being laid up at Barrow until the end of the year, Arnot Young & Company broke her up at Dalmuir in early 1972.

The new 'Lady' goes down the ways at Troon on 4th December 1975. *(IOMSPCo)*

THE MANX FLEET IN 1976

The new *Lady of Mann* was the fourth of a quartette of side-loading car ferries. The design principle for vehicle loading was simple - a spiral set of ramps at the stern linked with the car deck so that vehicles could be driven on or off at the appropriate level. This overcame the difficulty of the twenty foot tidal range at Douglas. At Liverpool the car deck was on the level with the landing stage. This system of inclined ramps was devised by the Company's Superintendent Engineer, the late Mr C J Kenna. The system had been used at least once before on the Belgian car ferry *London-Istanbul* (ex *Ville de Liege*), introduced onto the Dover to Ostend route in 1936.

The Steam Packet Company's first side-loading car ferry was the

The ***Lady of Mann*** arrives at Douglas from Troon shortly before 21.00 on 29th June 1976. *(Jenny Williamson)*

Manx Maid [2] of 1962. At the time the Company looked at the Clyde car ferries such as the *Glen Sannox* which used a hydraulic lift to lower cars to car deck level, but this system was painfully slow in operation and would have increased the turn-round times when full vehicle loads were carried in the summer. The side-loading car ferries were very versatile - they could successfully operate at any port where the vessel could get alongside and put the car ramp (carried on the vessel) on to the quay. The *Manx Maid* [2] was a turbine steamer, and in 1966 a sister vessel, the *Ben-my-Chree* [5] was added to the fleet.

In 1972 the motor vessel *Mona's Queen* was commissioned. At a time when other companies were moving towards roll on-roll off operations, it may seem strange that the Isle of Man Steam Packet Company chose to build a third side-loading car ferry. There were several reasons for this. Firstly, there was no linkspan at Douglas, nor were there any plans to provide one. Secondly, Douglas in the 1970s was an exposed open harbour and gales from an easterly point made the harbour unapproachable and set up a heavy swell causing vessels to 'range' alongside the quays. To illustrate this point it can be noted that during the winter of 1978-79 the Steam Packet diverted their vessel to Peel on the Island's west coast on eighteen occasions in easterly gale conditions. At Peel the side-loading car ferry could operate just as successfully as at Douglas. The Chairman of the Harbour Board stated that until Douglas harbour was fully protected from easterly gales by means of a breakwater extension, then no linkspan could be provided for ro-ro vessels. The third reason for

Maiden voyage. The 'Lady' leaves the North Edward Pier for Liverpool on 30th June 1976. *(W.S. Basnett)*

building a third side-loader was that it could operate perfectly satisfactorily from the Company's outports, such as Ardrossan or Belfast, or even Gourock when weather conditions made Ardrossan unapproachable.

The new *Lady of Mann* was a replacement for the passenger steamer *King Orry* [4] which was retired from service at the end of the 1975 season. The conditions which prevailed four years earlier when the *Mona's Queen* entered service had not changed: there were no plans to provide a linkspan at Douglas, and the harbour remained open and exposed to the east.

Accommodation for passengers on the new 'Lady' was "in the best traditions of the Isle of Man Steam Packet Company", that is, somewhat spartan but generally adequate for a four hour daylight voyage. There were passenger lounges forward on both the promenade and shelter decks. Amidships were the dining saloon and the bar. Beneath the car deck were situated the ladies' lounge and a sleeping lounge. Sixteen two-berth private cabins were provided. On each side of the promenade and shelter decks the Company's time honoured wooden bench seating was provided. The open deck spaces were of metal - there was no wooden cladding.

In 1976, when the new *Lady of Mann* joined the Steam Packet fleet, Manx tourism was enjoying something of a mini-boom. In 1975 the seven ship passenger fleet had carried 909,556 passengers; the highest total for very many years and one which has not been exceeded since, nor is it ever likely to be. In the 'Lady's' first year of operation the fleet carried 872,037 passengers, still well in excess of the average carryings of 802,000 per annum in the preceding ten years. By 1984 the combined Liverpool and Heysham passenger total amounted to 197,000; whilst in 1985 just 170,000 passengers were conveyed from Heysham.

Lady of Mann, post 1989. (I.O.M.S.P. Co.)

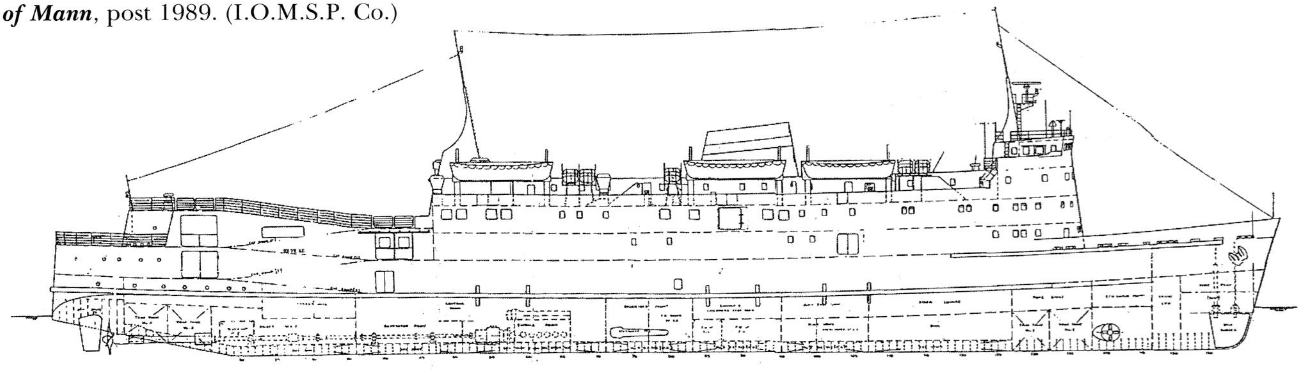

Maiden voyage. The 'Lady' arrives at the Liverpool Landing Stage on 30th June 1976. Notice the all yellow funnel which the ship carried early in her career. *(John Shepherd collection)*

The *Lady of Mann* joined a seven ship passenger fleet, all of which had been purpose-built to Steam Packet specifications. The other units were the *Mona's Queen* [5] - 1972, *Ben-my-Chree* [5] - 1966, *Manx Maid* [2] - 1962, *Manxman* [2] - 1955, *Mona's Isle* [5] - 1951 and *Snaefell* [5] - 1948. There were two cargo vessels - the *Peveril* [3] of 1963 and the *Conister* [2] of 1955. The *Conister* had been built as the *Brentfield* of Zillah Shipping and in 1959 became the *Spaniel* of the Coast Lines Group. The Steam Packet acquired her in November 1973, after a six month charter. Both vessels had been converted to cellular container ships by the Ailsa Shipbuilding Company at Troon.

In 1976 the Company's principal route was from Liverpool to Douglas. Seasonal services were operated to Fleetwood, Ardrossan, Belfast, Dublin and Llandudno. The Company also operated the Liverpool to Llandudno excursion service, taken over from the Liverpool & North Wales Steamship Company in 1963. Occasional charters were also operated, from ports such as Workington or Barrow. With the exception of the Llandudno services, the new 'Lady' operated on all the Company's routes.

In the mid 1970s, a crew would join a Steam Packet ship at the start of the season and remain with her until the winter lay up. There were no relief crews and 'days off', even at the height of the season, when the vessel would remain at Douglas, were common. Services were provided with the convenience of the passenger in mind, generally operated within social hours. Winter services were worked with a two ship operation - one vessel leaving Douglas at 09.00, and the other departing from Liverpool at 11.00, six days per week. For almost nine months out of every twelve, five of the passenger vessels were laid up in the Morpeth Dock, Birkenhead.

This was the situation in 1976 when the new *Lady of Mann* entered service. It hadn't altered much over the years, and there seemed no reason at all to change anything in the foreseeable future. To all intents and purposes the Isle of Man Steam Packet Company appeared 'timeless'. When other ferry operators were seeking to make economies in the inflationary 1970s, the Company carried on as before.

The 'Lady' had a successful first season, and returned to her builders at Troon for her guarantee overhaul in February 1977.

MANX LINE AND THE MERGER

The first hint that a major shake up of shipping patterns to the Isle of Man could be in the offing came in January 1977 when the Chairman of the Island's Harbour Board announced that roll on-roll off facilities were being considered by his Board, but their provision depended on two major factors: (1) the building of a breakwater extension likely to cost about £5 million, and (2) the provision of a linkspan which might require another £2 million. Meanwhile the Steam Packet fleet settled down to another routine year with the new 'Lady' sailing under the command of Commodore John Kennaugh. Traffic levels continued to be buoyant in this "Indian Summer" of Manx tourism.

Later in 1977 the Manx Government agreed to the expenditure of £650,000 to support the setting up of a ro-ro service which would operate in direct competition with the Steam Packet Company. This

On board the ***Lady of Mann*** in 1979. *Above*: The upper forward lounge. *Below*: The Dining Room. *(Both W.S. Basnett)*

sum would cover approximately half the cost of a linkspan installation in Douglas harbour. With the threat of a new operator commencing on Isle of Man routes in 1978, the Steam Packet Board decided to reduce the fleet to six ships and the thirty year old *Snaefell* was offered for sale at the end of the season.

The *Lady of Mann* partnered the *Mona's Queen* on the winter schedules, with the *Ben-my-Chree* deputising when the motorships were off for annual overhaul.

The Manx Line was formed in 1978 by a group of Island businessmen with the intention of providing a long overdue roll on-roll off service to the Isle of Man. The new company would use Heysham as its UK port with its existing linkspan and a 'MacGregor "F" type' linkspan was built at No 1 berth on the Victoria Pier at Douglas. It should be remembered that the Steam Packet abandoned the Heysham route as being unprofitable at the end of the 1974 season but the Manx Line purchased the Aznar Line vessel *Monte Castillo* to operate the modified service. The ship was duly renamed *Manx Viking*.

The new company was accepting bookings up to late May when it suddenly announced that its service would not in fact be running before 1st July at the earliest as the *Manx Viking* was strikebound in a Leith shipyard. The Steam Packet swiftly had to organise extra sailings at extremely short notice to carry the Manx Line TT Race traffic and the *Lady of Mann* and the five other members of the fleet had a very hectic fortnight.

On 15th August 1978 the *Lady of Mann* crossed from Fleetwood to Douglas in a berth to berth time of 2 hrs 39 mins, and the next day in 2 hrs 40 mins. Despite being very fast passages they were still 17 minutes slower than the *Viking's* record passage in 1905.

After months of delay the first Manx Line sailing from Heysham

Above: The 'Lady' slipping out of Douglas into a morning haze. *(W.S. Basnett)*

Below: During March 1979 the 'Lady' visited Manchester Dry Docks for annual survey. She is seen here on passage to Pomona Dock. *(W.S. Basnett)*

A superb bird's eye view of the ***Lady of Mann*** seen from the heights of Spanish Head, in the south of the Isle of Man. *(Jean Kinley)*

took place on 26th August 1978. A fortnight later one of the *Manx Viking's* diesel engines broke a piston, and sailings were again suspended. Once again the Manx Line traffic had to be transferred to the Steam Packet and the 'Lady' was kept busy running extra sailings.

The first severe easterly gale of the 1978-79 winter occurred on the night of 1st December and the Manx Line Victoria Pier linkspan broke adrift and caused considerable damage to the pier. Just under two years earlier, in January 1977, the Harbour Board Chairman had said that a pre-requisite for siting a linkspan in Douglas harbour was the construction of an extension to the Battery Pier breakwater to protect the harbour from easterly gales. In their haste to assist the new Manx Line this advice had been ignored by the Government, and the result was plain for all to see on the morning of 2nd December.

Without the linkspan the *Manx Viking* was unable to operate and was despatched to Belfast. The *Lady of Mann* and the *Mona's Queen* continued to provide the Island's lifeline with total reliability, using Peel whenever it was necessary due to stress of the weather. The Steam Packet heaved a sigh of relief and considered the Manx Line operation finished.

1979 was Millennium Year in the Isle of Man, celebrating 1,000 years of the Island's parliament, Tynwald. It was also the swansong for the Manx tourist industry and an extensive programme of events encouraged tourists to the Island, with the Steam Packet operating over 2,000 passenger sailings during the year.

The *Manx Viking* arrived back on the Heysham-Douglas service in May 1979 and the replacement linkspan was in position on the Victoria Pier in July when the full roll on-roll off Manx Line service was restored.

The years 1980-1984 proved to be very difficult for the Isle of Man Steam Packet Company. There is barely enough traffic on Isle of Man routes to support one operator for nine months of the year, let alone two, and at times the Manx Line (by now Sealink Manx Line) was charging wholly uneconomic fares. The Steam Packet sold the 'classic' steamer *Mona's Isle* at the end of the 1980 season, and the final 'classic' passenger-only steamer *Manxman* was disposed of two years later. This left the *Lady of Mann* and the three earlier car ferries to maintain the Company's services against a background of rapidly declining visitors to the Island. In order to effect economies, the hulls of the four car ferries were grit-blasted down to bare steel in 1982, and then seven coats of self-polishing paint were applied to give a very smooth surface which, with the passage of time, would get even smoother and thereby reduce resistance. Sailing times were rescheduled and a computer supplied timings and courses which allowed for wind and tide.

In the early 1980s the breakwater extension was constructed to protect Douglas harbour from easterly gales, and in June 1981 the Steam Packet brought its own linkspan into operation on the south side of the King Edward Pier. The chartered vessel *NF Jaguar* maintained the Steam Packet's own ro-ro service to Liverpool. The Company recorded trading losses in 1981 and 1982.

Against this depressed background the *Lady of Mann* soldiered on, helping to maintain a double-daily service to Liverpool during the

In July 1979, the 'Lady' is seen entering Douglas with a good complement of passengers enjoying the summer sun. *(L. Schofield)*

summer months, along with sailings to Belfast, Dublin, Ardrossan and Fleetwood. The Irish traffic from Dublin was buoyant, but the numbers on the midweek Liverpool sailings were pathetically low at times.

The UK Government sold Sealink (of which Manx Line was a part) to Sea Containers Limited on 27th July 1984 as part of its privatisation programme, and Sea Containers' entrepreneurial President, James Sherwood, arrived on the Manx shipping scene.

Matters were coming to a head in the autumn of 1984 with another loss seemingly inevitable for the Steam Packet. The steam turbine car ferries *Manx Maid* and *Ben-my-Chree* were offered for sale in October, and the Company announced that it had purchased the ro-ro vessel *Tamira*, formerly Townsend Thoresen's *Free Enterprise III*. The vessel was lying at Malta and Captain Vernon Kinley sailed her to

The year 1980 saw the Steam Packet celebrate their first 150 years. The timetable showed the *Lady of Mann* and her five fleet companions.

the Clyde under her new name of *Mona's Isle* [6] for complete refurbishment.

The traditional two ship winter service finished at the end of December 1984 with the *Lady of Mann* taking the final 11.00 sailing from Liverpool to Douglas. From January 1985 the 'Lady' sailed on alone with a 09.00 sailing from Douglas and a 14.30 return from Liverpool whilst the *Mona's Queen* received her annual overhaul. The appearance of the two motorships was not improved by the appearance of six foot high yellow lettering proclaiming "Isle of Man Steam Packet" along each side of the black hull.

Six years of competition from Sealink Manx Line led to a merger of the respective operations from 1st April 1985. However on the eve of the merger the situation was far from being auspicious: the Steam Packet's new flagship *Mona's Isle* was still at Govan with problems to her fire sprinkler system; the *Peveril* (ex *NF Jaguar*) was strikebound at Liverpool; the *Antrim Princess* wasn't available from Sealink to replace the *Manx Viking* whose survey certificates were due to expire within 24 hours. To compound matters the Heysham linkspan was blockaded by the crew of the *Stena Sailor*. Against this desperate situation the *Lady of Mann* and the *Mona's Queen* sailed a basic service to Heysham north quay, Liverpool having been abandoned altogether. Once again the reliability and versatility of the two remaining side-loading car ferries was tested to the full.

The 1985 summer season lurched from crisis to crisis as the new *Mona's Isle* had serious deadweight problems and could not carry anything like the load expected of her. At the Steam Packet Board Meeting of 15th August it was announced that she would be permanently withdrawn on 5th October after only six months in service. The *Antrim Princess* (on charter from Sealink) would replace her. The 'Lady' and the 'Queen' had saved the day yet again in 1985 carrying out their own programme of sailings and covering for and duplicating the *Mona's Isle's* sailings whenever necessary - which was most of the time.

THE ROAD TO RECOVERY

The *Tynwald* (ex *Antrim Princess*) and the *Manx Viking* ran the main Heysham service in 1986 with the two side-loaders operating the secondary services and backing up the Heysham route as required. The *Lady of Mann* appeared for Easter 1986 looking very smart and all the better for a complete absence of logos which had adorned her hull for the previous three years. She operated the 10.00 from Heysham on Thursday 27th March and at 14.30 sailed to Dublin before bringing in two Irish charters (at 20.00 Thursday and 09.30 Friday). She returned the Dublin charters at 20.00 (Monday 31st March) and 14.00 (Tuesday 1st April) and left Douglas at 11.00 on Wednesday, 2nd April to resume her lay up at Birkenhead.

The *Lady of Mann's* summer season started on Friday 9th May

Arriving in the River Lagan at Belfast from Peel in May 1984. *(Rodney McKenna)*

1986 with a Dublin-Douglas charter which she returned on Sunday 11th May. On Tuesday 13th May she operated an educational day trip from Greenore to Douglas and there was a "Round the Island" cruise on Sunday 18th May. Following the Greenore sailings, the 'Lady' crossed 'light' to Heysham to duplicate the *Manx Viking's* 01.30 sailing on Thursday 15th May. The 'Viking' was carrying hazardous cargo and the passengers were carried on the *Lady of Mann*. This was always a problem when mixing passengers and freight, but it was a situation that would be resolved in the autumn when the *Manx Viking* would be withdrawn, and the freight only ro-ro vessel *Peveril* would take her place.

The 'Lady' opened the scheduled Liverpool service on Tuesday 20th May 1986. After having abandoned Liverpool altogether on 30th March 1985, a limited service was offered for the summer only of 1986. Liverpool has always been the natural port of departure for the Isle of Man, and the transfer of services to Heysham has only served to alienate many loyal passengers. In violent gales on Tuesday 27th May, the *Lady of Mann* operated the Liverpool service with no delays, whilst the Heysham service was suspended for some hours.

In 1978 the Douglas to Dublin service had at last been accepted by the Customs and Excise as foreign-going and the Steam Packet Company were permitted to sell duty-free goods. With no suitable facilities available on board, a specially constructed trailer was driven on to the car ramps of the Dublin bound vessel to act as a makeshift duty-free shop. However over the 1985-1986 winter a duty-free supermarket was built into the *Lady of Mann* in the former ladies' lounge, and as far as possible the 'Lady' became the regular Dublin vessel.

On Tuesday 26th August 1986, the tail end of 'Hurricane Charlie' came up the Irish Sea. The 'Lady' was stormbound in Heysham all day, finally sailing at 17.45. Her 08.20 Liverpool sailing departed at 22.00 that evening, and the 14.30 Liverpool-Douglas left at 03.00 Wednesday 27th. The 'Lady' closed the Belfast route on Sunday 14th September, operated relief sailings to Heysham on Monday 15th September, closed the seasonal Dublin service on Wednesday 17th September and docked at Birkenhead on Thursday 18th September.

A special programme of October sailings was operated by the *Lady of Mann*. She undocked on Thursday 23rd with a Liverpool-Douglas sailing and the following day sailed to Dublin at 10.00, returning with a charter. A planned Douglas to Liverpool day excursion on Saturday, 25th October was cancelled as the 'Lady' was stormbound all day, and on Sunday 26th a day excursion to Fleetwood was offered in connection with the Blackpool Illuminations. 600 passengers with 60 cars took advantage of this sailing. The 'Lady' returned her charter to Dublin on 27th October, returned with a public sailing to Douglas and then left for Liverpool with another public sailing on Tuesday 28th October, after which she redocked at Birkenhead.

The *Manx Viking* was duly disposed of to Norwegian interests at the end of September 1986 and the *Tynwald* maintained the passenger services, whilst the *Peveril* operated the freight sailings. The *Mona's Queen* covered for the *Tynwald's* annual overhaul.

ROUND THE ISLAND

The *Lady of Mann* returned to Douglas from Birkenhead on Thursday 30th April 1987 to commence her summer season. Dublin charters kept her busy initially along with a charter day excursion to Liverpool on Saturday 2nd May. The 'Lady' provided duplicate sailings with the *Tynwald* for the Manx Car Rally traffic between Thursday 14th and Sunday, 17th May. On Bank Holiday Monday 25th May both the *Lady of Mann* and the *Mona's Queen* worked the 14.00 sailing to Liverpool; the first time that two Steam Packet vessels had been together alongside the landing stage since September 1984.

The return rush of TT traffic started in earnest on Friday 5th June with the 'Lady' sailing from Douglas every eleven hours and returning light. Bad weather and the fact that the Friday Race was postponed until Saturday caused problems and sailings were running up to three hours behind schedule. After the TT traffic was over the *Mona's Queen* docked at Birkenhead and laid up until 2nd July with the *Lady of Mann* operating the side-loader sailings single-handed and opening the Stranraer route on Thursday, 11th June - her first ever visit to the Scottish port. The 'Lady' operated the Tynwald Day special excursion

Alongside at Liverpool at Easter 1986. *(John Shepherd)*

from Douglas to Fleetwood on 6th July.

On Sunday 30th August the *Lady of Mann* operated a Round-the-Island Charity Cruise, when over 1,000 passengers enjoyed a perfect evening cruise. End of season duties were changed at the very last minute when the 'Lady' developed bow thrust problems. After working the 08.45 to Heysham on Monday 14th September, she returned to Douglas to destore and entered the Langton drydock at Liverpool on Wednesday 16th, subsequently moving to the Bidston Dock at Birkenhead for lay up. Consequently the *Mona's Queen* took over the 'Lady's' schedules.

The *Lady of Mann* was on duty again between 23rd and 26th October working weekend trips to Dublin, and day excursions to

Liverpool and Fleetwood; a very similar programme to that operated in 1986. The weather was kind and the full weekend programme ran to schedule. Meanwhile the *Mona's Queen* was being overhauled alongside the north Edward Pier at Douglas - the new breakwater extension was thought to provide sufficient shelter to make this possible. It was the intention to similarly overhaul the 'Lady' at Douglas between Easter and May 1988.

REDUCED CERTIFICATE

The *Mona's Queen* and the *Lady of Mann* had their passenger certificates reduced from 1,600 to 1,200 in early 1988. This was a result of revised manning regulations, introduced following the Zeebrugge disaster. The 'Lady' left drydock at Birkenhead on 12th April.

During the afternoon of Friday 29th April 1988 the National Union of Seamen went on strike in support of the P&O men at Dover. All Steam Packet services were stopped until Saturday 14th May. The Manx Stages Car Rally was cancelled and grave concern was felt for the TT Races. Accordingly the Isle of Man Department of Tourism chartered the *Bolette* from Fred Olsen Line from 25th May until 12th June at a cost in excess of £1 million, in order to safeguard the Races. (The *Bolette* was the former *Viking 5*). The charter went ahead despite settlement of the NUS dispute.

The *Lady of Mann* sailed light from Birkenhead to Douglas on Monday 23rd May and on the following day opened the Liverpool route for the summer. The same day the *Tynwald* developed bow thruster problems and did not sail: the 'Lady' took her sailings after arriving back in Douglas from Liverpool.

The Liverpool 'shuttle' TT sailings were operated by the *Lady of Mann*. Between Thursday 2nd June and Saturda, 4th June she worked six round trips; in service ex Liverpool and 'light' from Douglas. The homeward 'shuttle' involved seven round trips from 20.00 on Thursday 9th June to 20.15 on Saturday 12th June.

The Heysham linkspan was out of service on 6th and 7th June, and the 'Lady' covered the *Tynwald's* sailings, once again saving the situation. A similar situation existed on 4th July and the 'Lady' operated to Heysham using the north berth, whilst the *Tynwald* was despatched to Belfast for the day.

The *Mona's Queen* was laid up after the TT period until Sunday 3rd July, and the *Lady of Mann* took all the side-loader sailings. The 'Lady' carried a capacity crowd to Fleetwood on Tynwald Day, 5th July 1988.

Severe gales blew up on the night of Sunday 24th July and on arrival at Douglas on Monday morning the *Tynwald* (01.30 from Heysham) came into contact with the 'Lady' and subsequently burst a large 'balloon' fender which became entangled in her propellers. Due to the storm Monday's Heysham sailings were cancelled whilst the 'Lady's' Belfast and Liverpool sailings were at first delayed and then cancelled. The *Tynwald* was sent to Birkenhead for drydocking and the 'Lady' and the 'Queen' deputised. The *Lady of Mann* was alongside the landing stage at Liverpool on Monday 8th August with the Royal Yacht *Britannia*.

The *Lady of Mann* closed the Belfast service on 18th September and Dublin on 21st September. Severe gales caused the *Tynwald's* sailings to be cancelled on Friday, 23rd September, although by early afternoon conditions were sufficiently improved for the 'Lady' to operate substitute sailings to Liverpool at 14.00 with a 19.15 return, passengers being "bussed" to and from Heysham.

On Monday 26th September the increasingly unreliable *Tynwald* broke down at Heysham and had to proceed to Birkenhead for emergency drydocking. The *Lady of Mann*, which had only docked for the winter the previous day, was hastily brought out and resumed service with the 01.30 from Heysham on Tuesday 27th September. She continued to work the passenger service until the *Tynwald's* return on 29th September.

There was no programme of October half-term sailings in 1988, and it was announced that the *Lady of Mann* was to receive a complete rebuild in early 1989. Portland Design Associates of London were responsible for the interior work. The 'Lady's' basic passenger accommodation was simply not acceptable in the late 1980s and it urgently needed to be brought up to a standard similar to that provided by other operators.

MAJOR REBUILD

The rebuilding of the *Lady of Mann* was the largest job ever undertaken by Wright and Beyer at Birkenhead. Completion was scheduled for mid-April. By mid-February 1989 the hull and funnel had been grit-blasted and red-leaded, most of the original passenger accommodation had been gutted, and the side passenger doors on the shelter deck had been replaced by sheet metal.

By 2nd May much work still needed to be done on board the 'Lady', both internally and externally. A large circular motif appeared on her forward superstructure beneath the wheelhouse. The 'Lady' was due to be recommissioned in Douglas on Friday 19th and to re-enter service on 26th May, but the work was not complete. Her celebration Douglas-Peel trips on 20th and 21st May, and the subsequent promotional visits to Londonderry, Belfast and Dublin

Captain Kinley bringing the 'Lady' up the Wyre past the stranded No. 13 buoy on dead low water at Fleetwood during the 1993 season. *(Captain Tom Harrison)*

were cancelled.

After a reception in Liverpool, the *Lady of Mann* returned to service with the 19.00 Liverpool-Douglas sailing on Friday 26th May, the rebuilt vessel also operating next day's Liverpool sailings. At a ceremony in Douglas on Sunday 28th May she was officially recommissioned by Mrs Norman Corlett, the wife of the Company's Chairman. At 19.00 the 'Lady' operated an evening cruise to the Calf of Mann, which included diversions into Port St Mary Bay (turning off the Alfred Pier), and into Port Erin Bay (turning to the landward side of the ruined breakwater), and then proceeding as far north as Laxey before returning to Douglas.

The *Lady of Mann's* refit was very impressive. "A" Deck was the Boat Deck, and previously metal decks had been timber-clad. This deck contained the officers' accommodation and new passenger cabins. "B" Deck, the old promenade deck, was the main passenger deck with lounges, the information bureau, a shop, toilets and the promenade cafe. All the seating was luxurious, the whole area being finished in pastel shades of blue, green and pink. "C" Deck, the original shelter deck, had more lounge accommodation, the "Triskale" Bar (which had no natural light and was consequently claustrophobic), the baggage room, more toilets and the upper car deck where some 30 cars could be stowed. "D" Deck was the main car deck, and "E" Deck had the duty-free shop, the cinema and a family room. This family room was the only accommodation unaltered from earlier times.

The 'Lady's' gross tonnage increased from 2,990 to 3,176 and she was licensed to carry 950 passengers and 50 crew on a temporary certificate covering the period 26th May to 23rd June 1989.

After taking the Dublin sailings on Wednesday 14th June (where she was open to the travel trade), the *Lady of Mann* sailed from Douglas to Liverpool at 09.00 on Thursday 15th and then went back to Wright & Beyer at Birkenhead for the completion of the refit, in particular finishing the new cabins on the boat deck. With her refit finally complete, and with a certificate for 1,000 passengers, the 'Lady' arrived back in Douglas on Friday 7th July and resumed service with that morning's 09.15 to Dublin.

On Wednesday 26th July the *Lady of Mann* operated the Fleetwood 'funboat' excursion and had to leave 200 passengers behind due to her lesser capacity than the *Mona's Queen*. On Tuesday 8th August the 'Lady' had 138 cars on board on a sailing from Liverpool - an all-time record for a sideloader. It should be remembered that as well as using the main garage deck, vehicles were stowed on the spiral ramps at the stern. This practice was not always appreciated by car owners when the weather was rough as their vehicles would arrive drenched in salt spray!

The ageing and unreliable *Tynwald* was off-duty again with engine trouble from Tuesday 15th August until Saturday, 19th August and it was left to the two side-loaders to operate the main Heysham service, along with all the secondary services.

After taking the Douglas to Fleetwood sailing on Wednesday 30th August 1989, the *Mona's Queen* left the Lancashire port early on 31st August and sailed directly to Cherbourg, arriving at 18.00 on Friday 1st September. She had been chartered by the French post office, and

Right: The 'Lady' covered in red-lead during the period of her major refurbishment in February 1989. *(John Shepherd)*

Another atmospheric Fleetwood view with the ***Lady of Mann*** arriving to take the morning departure to Douglas. *(Captain Vernon Kinley)*

sailed to the Solent to view the start of the Round the World Yacht Race in which their yacht, *La Poste*, was participating. On Sunday 3rd September the 'Queen' was chartered by Sealink to deputise for the *Earl Granville*, and had a further spell of charter work at Weymouth until 23rd September.

With the *Mona's Queen* away, the 'Lady' and the *Tynwald* had a busy time coping with the two ship Manx Grand Prix and car rally schedules during the first nine days of September. The *Lady of Mann's* last Dublin trip of the year on Wednesday 20th September was disrupted by storm force winds; after being at sea for three hours the 'Lady' was forced to turn back off the Calf and return to Douglas. The sailing was then postponed until 20.00 that evening.

The *Lady of Mann* operated an "Illuminations Special" on Sunday 24th September leaving Douglas for Fleetwood at 10.00, and returning from the Lancashire port at 22.30. Four days later, on 28th September, the 'Lady' laid up in the Alexandra Dock, Liverpool. The Mersey Docks and Harbour Company said that the usual lay-up berth at Vittoria Dock, in Birkenhead, was required for redevelopment and was not available. The Steam Packet was very unhappy with the Alexandra Dock arrangements, and was said to be seriously considering using Belfast for future years.

Charter sailings disturbed the *Lady of Mann's* winter slumbers in December. From Thursday 21st until Saturday 23rd December, the 'Lady' went on charter to the B&I Line to deputise for the *Norrona*, which was off service with storm damage. The 'Lady' operated double daily sailings between Holyhead and Dublin, running in conjunction with the Irish ferry *Leinster*.

THE *CHANNEL ENTENTE* JOINS THE FLEET

On 7th February 1990 the Steam Packet Company obtained approval from its shareholders to purchase the multi-purpose vessel *Channel Entente* (formerly the train ferry *Saint Eloi*). After stringent berthing trials at all the Steam Packet's ports, the new vessel replaced the *Tynwald* on the main Heysham route from Monday 19th February.

From Friday 9th February 1990 the *Lady of Mann* returned to Holyhead on charter to Sealink to cover for the fire damaged *St Columba* on the Holyhead-Dun Laoghaire route. The 'Lady' (passengers, cars and mail) and the *St Cybi* (freight) partnered each other until 7th March, when the *Horsa* replaced the 'Lady'.

The *Lady of Mann* commenced her Easter sailings on Wednesday 11th April with a single passage from Holyhead to Dublin on charter to B&I to cover for the *Norrona* which was out of service following a fire. Following this she carried out a full programme of Steam Packet sailings to and from Liverpool, Belfast and Dublin. These finished on Wednesday 18th April after which 'the 'Lady' proceeded to Harland and Wolff at Belfast for her annual overhaul.

Fresh from her overhaul at Belfast, the *Lady of Mann* arrived back in Douglas on Monday 14th May and resumed service on Thursday 17th May. During the TT Race period the 'Lady' covered the Liverpool "shuttle" sailings in similar fashion to 1989.

The *Channel Entente* proved herself to be a very satisfactory vessel for the Steam Packet and in August it was announced that she would be given a major refurbishment at Birkenhead in the autumn of 1990. The *Channel Entente* and the recently rebuilt *Lady of Mann* had about as much car capacity as was available on the three passenger ships until recently and so the *Mona's Queen* would be laid up at the end of the season and her loss-making activities curtailed. The 'Queen's' last

In dry dock being made ready for another season. *(Captain Vernon Kinley)*

The Bar on C Deck following her 1989 rebuild. *(J.R.Clague)*

sailing was expected to be the 08.00 Douglas-Liverpool on Monday 3rd September; however on her previous trip, the 20.00 from Liverpool on Sunday evening, she suffered serious technical problems and eventually limped into Douglas on one engine at about 02.30. The Monday sailing then conveyed cars only, with the passengers sailing on the *Channel Entente* to Heysham and being "bussed" to Liverpool to be reunited with their cars. The 'Queen' entered Liverpool's Langton drydock that same afternoon for repairs.

The *Channel Entente* finished service on Wednesday 26th September and retired to Birkenhead's Bidston Dock for rebuilding. The 'Lady' was expected to work the Heysham service until Thursday 11th December, when the *King Orry* (ex *Channel Entente*) would resume. In an exclusive interview with "The Manx Independent", James Sherwood revealed Sea Containers' strategic thinking for the Steam Packet if control of the Company was gained. The Heysham route would be operated by two SeaCats, plus a large freight ro-ro vessel about twice the size of the *Peveril*. The *King Orry*, despite being recently refurbished, would be sold, and the *Lady of Mann* would be retained for the seasonal routes and supplementary Heysham sailings, or to cover when the SeaCats were stormbound.

The 'Lady' was herself stormbound at Heysham on Saturday 6th October and the 14.30 sailing did not leave until mid-morning on Sunday 7th. Over the Irish Bank Holiday weekend the *Lady of Mann* made 28 crossings between Wednesday 24th and Wednesday 31st October, ten of them between Dublin and Douglas, slotted in between the Heysham programme. Up to 1984, 28 sailings would have represented four and a half weeks' work for each of the vessels on winter service!

Saturday 8th December 1990 was extremely stormy: The 'Lady' sailed as usual from Douglas but became stormbound at Heysham, and did not sail until 06.30 on the Sunday morning. The refurbished *King Orry* had arrived back in Douglas on 6th December and after a recommissioning ceremony and being open for public viewing, she entered service with the 18.00 sailing to Heysham on Sunday evening, 9th December, her departure being marked by a fireworks display. The 'Lady' also left Douglas that Sunday evening - for lay up at Bidston Dock.

A TWO-SHIP PASSENGER FLEET

With the *Peveril* being overhauled in Canada drydock, Liverpool, the *Lady of Mann* departed Bidston Dock on Wednesday 2nd January 1991 and took over the passenger service the next morning. The *King Orry* then operated two round trips per day for freight. After a week of violent storms, the 'Lady' re-opened the winter Liverpool passenger service (Saturdays only) on 12th January in calm, sunny weather with 312 passengers and 70 cars. The *Peveril* returned to service on Tuesday 22nd January, but the *King Orry* then unexpectedly went into drydock with the 'Lady' remaining on the passenger service until 26th January.

The *King Orry* was off between Thursday 28th February and Wednesday, 6th March, having fouled a cable in her new bow thrust. Once again the 'Lady' was brought out of winter dock to operate the passenger service. It was almost possible to board the 'Lady', press the button, and sail away at a moment's notice! A one-ship operation (the *King Orry*) worked the Easter sailings in 1991.

One of the *Lady of Mann's* first sailings in the 1991 summer season was a charity cruise to Ramsey Bay on Sunday, 19th May. She had 500 passengers on board and she went alongside the south breakwater at Ramsey, the first Steam Packet passenger vessel to do so since before the Second World War. Passenger vessels called at Ramsey's Queen's Pier until 1970.

Following completion of her own summer sailings on Monday 16th September, the 'Lady' operated the Heysham route for a couple of days to give the *King Orry* time off for maintenance. In early October the *Mona's Queen* moved under her own power from Alexandra Dock in Liverpool to Vittoria Dock, Birkenhead (which was once again available), to lay up outside the 'Lady'. James Sherwood of Sea Containers suggested that the 'Lady' be chartered for part of each winter to replace the SeaCat on the Stranraer-Belfast service during the period of most severe weather!

ANNIVERSARY

The *Lady of Mann* left Birkenhead on Thursday 9th January 1992 and covered for the *King Orry's* overhaul period until Saturday 15th February. The 'Lady' visited Belfast on Monday 17th February to test the side-loading arrangements at the Company's new berth at Donegall Quay, after which she returned to lay up at Birkenhead. Her own drydocking and overhaul was complete by 30th April.

The month of May 1992 marked the 150th anniversary of the first IOMSP sailing between the Lancashire port of Fleetwood and Douglas. The first sailing was by the wooden paddle steamer *Mona's Isle* on 31st May 1842. The anniversary voyage was made on 24th May 1992 by the *Lady of Mann* under the command of Captain Vernon Kinley. The occasion was enough to merit a civic send-off from the Mayor of Fleetwood.

The 'Lady' looked immaculate, having only just re-entered service for the season. The 09.30 sailing was so well supported that boarding was not complete until 09.56 with 900 passengers. The 'Lady' was alongside No 4 Victoria Pier, Douglas, by 13.05. A special cruise to Peel left 37 minutes later with 600 passengers. There was some doubt about whether the wind conditions would allow a berth to be cleared at Peel, but Marine Superintendent Captain Peter Corrin arranged this. The occasion was almost certainly the last time that a Steam Packet vessel would berth at Peel. The 'Lady' arrived back at Douglas at 17.55 and sailed on the return passage to Fleetwood at 18.33, arriving at 21.57.

Following the peak TT Race week, the *King Orry* was withdrawn from service for 36 hours from Sunday, 7th June to undergo propeller repairs in Canada drydock, Liverpool. Meanwhile, the *Lady of Mann* operated around the clock, and only one sailing was cancelled.

The 'Lady' disgraced herself on Tuesday, 4th August whilst working the 20.30 Douglas to Fleetwood 'funboat' excursion with 300

The 'sisters' together in the Vittoria Dock at Birkenhead during April 1992. *(John Hendy)*

passengers. The unusually late departure from Douglas was due to tidal conditions at Fleetwood. She developed engine trouble and at 23.30 in deteriorating weather and running on one engine only, the decision was made to divert to Liverpool, where she arrived at 05.30 the next morning. There then appears to have been some difficulty in making arrangements to transport the passengers back to Fleetwood. Following repairs the 'Lady' returned light to Douglas and resumed service with that day's 14.00 Douglas to Liverpool, retimed to 18.00.

Whilst on passage from Dublin to Douglas on 10th September, the *Lady of Mann* became involved in an air-sea rescue search. She was a few miles out from Dublin when a passenger spotted a capsized yacht a short distance from the 'Lady'. Captain Kinley immediately alerted the Irish coastguard and was requested to search the surrounding area before being released to proceed to Douglas. Eight miles further on the 'Lady' was requested to return to the search area, but two hours later it was established that the yacht had actually sunk the previous week, but had only recently resurfaced. The 'Lady' eventually arrived at Douglas at 00.30, some two hours late.

Following her Belfast-Douglas-Liverpool sailing on Monday 14th September, the *Lady of Mann* moved 'light' to Barrow to work a special charter for Associated British Ports the following day. From 12.15 until 15.00 she cruised out to Lightning Knoll, the fairway buoy at the seaward end of Walney Channel, to celebrate the 125th anniversary of the port of Barrow. The 'Lady' then returned 'light' to Douglas to

Spot the difference : the 'Lady' and the 'Queen.' *(John Hendy)*

stand in for the *King Orry* on the Heysham run on 16th/17th September before docking at Birkenhead alongside a deteriorating *Mona's Queen*.

Whilst working the 18.15 Liverpool-Douglas sailing on Saturday 14th November, the *King Orry* suffered steering failure about three miles north of Formby Point and grounded on the Taylor's Bank just over an hour before low water. The 'Orry' was refloated at around 22.30 and towed back to Liverpool. The *Lady of Mann* was immediately reactivated and left Birkenhead's Vittoria Dock at 23.30 on Sunday 15th November and restored passenger services with a 02.30 sailing from Liverpool on the Monday morning. This conveyed the stranded Saturday passengers and also those from the 01.30 ex Heysham Monday morning sailing. The 'Lady' remained in service until the 08.15 Douglas-Liverpool sailing on Saturday 21st November.

"Lloyds List" announced that Sea Containers were planning to operate the seasonal Victoria (British Columbia) to Seattle (Washington State, USA) ferry after its closure by BC Stena Line in 1990. The *Lady of Mann* was earmarked for this route from the spring of 1993! To replace the 'Lady' on Manx routes, a SeaCat would be introduced! In the event the British Columbian government asked their own BC Ferry Corporation to take over the route, and the 'Lady' was consequently not required.

ROUND THE CLOCK SAILINGS

The *Lady of Mann* undocked on Friday 22nd January 1993 to relieve the *King Orry* for winter overhaul. On Saturday 23rd January the 'Lady' departed from Douglas for Liverpool on time, but for the second week running the day trippers would not be back until Sunday with the 18.15 return being delayed until 07.30 Sunday because of severe gales; the 'Lady' then taking over six hours on passage.

Much unfavourable comment has been made in the Isle of Man about sailings at unsocial hours, brought about by working a reduced fleet around the clock. Easter traffic was particularly badly hit. The *Lady of Mann* was brought out at Easter 1993 to provide extra Dublin sailings with the Manx Government Tourist Board financing any possible losses.

The *Lady of Mann's* 1993 summer season commenced on Wednesday 26th May with a cruise from Liverpool to Moelfre Bay (Anglesey) for the Battle of the Atlantic Review. In north-easterly force 8/9 conditions the 'Lady's' 492 passengers had a stormy eight hours and Captain Edward Fargher had to hold his ship on station with the engines as it was too rough to get an anchor hold in the appointed position. The next day the 'Lady' was alongside at Liverpool Pier Head, prior to her 19.30 departure for Douglas, dressed overall next to the Royal Yacht *Britannia*.

Passengers on the opening Fleetwood sailing of the season on Sunday 30th May were able to join an afternoon cruise to Port St Mary - the first time that the *Lady of Mann* had berthed there, before returning to Fleetwood at 18.30.

At 16.20 on Wednesday 2nd June, the *Lady of Mann* was manoeuvring in Douglas harbour on arrival from Liverpool with a full load of TT traffic. Instead of going astern into No 4 berth on the Victoria Pier, she surged ahead and smashed into the Battery Pier, as a result of the starboard main engine failing to respond correctly. This necessitated her withdrawal from service for 36 hours whilst temporary repairs were made. The timing of this accident could not have been worse as the TT traffic build-up was at its peak. To try and clear some of the backlog *SeaCat Scotland* made a single passage from

The ***Lady of Mann*** at Peel in May 1992. *(Brett Martin)*

Stranraer to Douglas, and Caledonian MacBrayne's *Pioneer* sailed from Gourock for Douglas. A temporary bulkhead was fitted forward of the bow thrust machinery before a temporary passenger certificate was issued to cover the 'Lady' over the TT period.

On completion of the TT traffic, the *Lady of Mann* was sent to the Mersey for permanent repair by Wright and Beyer on 15th June, and returned to service with the midnight sailing on 21st June (re-timed from the scheduled 19.00 departure).

The final Fleetwood sailing of the season departed at 07.15 on 7th September. This gave over eight hours ashore to join the centenary celebrations of the Manx Electric Railway, before sailing for Fleetwood at 20.00.

The remainder of the 1993 summer season passed off without further incident and the 'Lady' docked at Birkenhead on Monday 20th September.

REPLACED BY THE SEACAT

The *Lady of Mann* re-entered passenger service on Friday 7th January 1994, covering for the *King Orry's* overhaul period. Gales on Thursday 27th January caused the 'Lady' to remain in Douglas all day. On Thursday 3rd February she took almost seven hours to reach Heysham, the 14.00 return being cancelled. The 'Lady' resumed with the 14.00 from Heysham the following day. The *King Orry* returned to service on Saturday 5th February when the 'Lady' sailed back to Birkenhead's Vittoria Dock and berthed alongside the redundant *Mona's Queen*.

On 11th March 1994 a statement was released on the Stock Exchange Regulatory News Service stating that a high speed craft was to be deployed on Manx routes from mid-June to September, replacing the *Lady of Mann*. The 'Lady' would remain as back-up for the SeaCat until the end of the season, berthed at Birkenhead. So the situation was that the Isle of Man Steam Packet Company was ridding itself of a recently refurbished, well-tried and excellent sea boat which was able to cope with almost anything that the Irish Sea could throw at her. In her place came a high technology SeaCat with limited capacity and only able to operate in wave heights of up to 3.5 metres.

The *Lady of Mann* commenced what was thought to be her final season on 26th May. She covered the sailings advertised for her in the Company's sailing brochure until the end of June. The 'Lady' made

On 28th May 1993, the 'Lady' shared the Pier Head with the Royal Yacht *Britannia*. *(J.R. Clague)*

her final Fleetwood crossings on 21st June with over 800 passengers. Her final passenger sailing was from Liverpool at 19.00 on Monday 27th June. The next morning she left Douglas 'light ship' for Liverpool at 08.00. There were siren exchanges with the *King Orry* in harbour, and then the *Lady of Mann* swept majestically around Douglas Bay, just as her namesake had done some 23 years earlier. She berthed in the Vittoria Dock at Birkenhead at the same time as *SeaCat Isle of Man* was making its inaugural Fleetwood-Douglas crossing.

There were persistent rumours about a future for the *Lady of Mann* on the Irish Sea. A Fleetwood and Dublin passenger and vehicle service was proposed. An unknown source wanted to operate the 'Lady' between Liverpool and the old B&I Jetfoil berth at Dublin. It was announced at the end of the year that *SeaCat Isle of Man* had carried 33% more passengers in July and August than the *Lady of Mann* had carried in the corresponding period in 1993.

CHARTER WORK IN MADEIRA

The *Lady of Mann* undocked from Birkenhead on the morning of 1st February 1995 and sailed 'light' to Heysham, where she swapped over with the *King Orry* to cover the passenger sailings during the 'Orry's' annual overhaul period. The 'Lady' continued in service until Thursday 9th March.

A new company, styled Liver Ferries, set a start-up date for a new Liverpool-Dublin service of 3rd April 1995, using the *Lady of Mann*.

On 30th May 1993 the 'Lady' was alongside at Port St. Mary. *(J.R. Clague)*

Nothing more came of this venture and the 'Lady' appeared for the intensive TT period on 26th May. She had been surveyed afloat and whilst her external appearance could have been improved with the use of a paint brush, internally she was as immaculate as ever. Captain Alan Bridson was in command for her brief eighteen day outing which concentrated on Liverpool sailings, but which also included Fleetwood on 28th May, Heysham on 5th June and Belfast on 11th June. Many of the crew were Steam Packet 'veterans'.

The *Lady of Mann* left Douglas at 12.00 on Monday, 12th June with the remnants of the returning TT traffic. It was a fairly slow passage and she passed the Rock Light at New Brighton at 15.50 before berthing at the landing stage some twenty minutes later. After discharging she left for the Vittoria Dock at Birkenhead and berthed alongside her sister, the *Mona's Queen*.

The 'Queen' had been laid up for four years and ten months despite interest intermittently being shown in her. At one stage she was earmarked for a new Folkestone-Boulogne service, and more recently a prospective Greek buyer had put down, and subsequently forfeited, a £100,000 deposit on her. Her engines were satisfactorily tested in early 1995.

After lying in the Vittoria Dock with the *Mona's Queen* for a month, the *Lady of Mann* was moved to the Bidston drydock where her underwater hull received attention and paint.

Charter work for the *Lady of Mann* had been arranged in Madeira. A Portuguese crew duly arrived in Birkenhead and with Captain Vernon Kinley acting as undocking pilot, the ship cleared the Alfred Locks at 14.45 on 17th June 1995.

The *Lady of Mann* berthed at the Liverpool landing stage from 15.35 until 17.25 to take on bunkers for the passage to Madeira after

On the Boat Deck. *(John Hendy)*

which she passed the Rock Light outward bound at 17.40 and hove to at the Mersey Bar to drop her pilot at 18.15. Soon the familiar silhouette was underway again heading for the Orme's Head and the Skerries off Anglesey, before turning south and setting course for Madeira. The 'Lady' arrived at Funchal, Madeira's capital on 21st July after a four day reduced speed (16 knots) passage.

The *Lady of Mann* duly took up service on the Madeira to Porto Santo route although her schedule was not particularly demanding. Leaving Funchal (Madeira) at 08.00 each morning, she berthed to Vila Baleira (Porto Santo) at 10.15. The returning sailing departed at 18.00 with arrival at Funchal timed at 20.15. Occasional sailings to the Canary Islands were planned although the 'Lady's' suitability for a 200 mile 10 hour passage in the Atlantic Ocean was certainly doubtful.

The ship's initial charter was for three months with an option to extend this by a further month. The charterers were PS Line, a subsidiary of a long-established Madeira company with which arrangements to operate the Porto Santo service had been made with the Portuguese Government.

UNCERTAIN FUTURE

At this stage in her career, the future of the *Lady of Mann* could only be described as 'uncertain.' In mid-September 1995, the Isle of Man Steam Packet Company announced a pre-tax loss of £107,000 for the first half of the year, much of this being attributable to the unfortunate Mannin Line episode and the £6,000 a day charter fee of the *SeaCat Isle of Man*. The Company stated that it wished to dispose of both the Mannin Line vessel *Belard* and the *Lady of Mann* as soon as possible.

Two days after this announcement, on Wednesday 27th September, an unfortunate incident occurred which may have handed the 'Lady' a much-needed lifeline. The *King Orry* was in dry-dock in Liverpool for a few days and the *SeaCat Isle of Man* was operating the Douglas - Heysham service. In the first moderate north westerly gale of the autumn the SeaCat left Douglas for Heysham but was diverted to Liverpool on passage. A delayed return crossing to the island commenced at 20.00 but some forty minutes out, near the Formby Light Float in the Crosby Channel, the vessel was struck by a large wave which damaged her bow-visor. The craft was immediately returned to Liverpool and taken out of service, passengers being accommodated in local hotels until the *King Orry* was hastily recalled to service on the following afternoon.

All other routes around the U.K. operated by SeaCats or similar craft have back-up in the form of conventional vessels. On 27th September the conditions in Liverpool Bay were only moderate - a force 6 to 7 which the *Lady of Mann* would have taken in her stride.

After much deliberation, it was finally decided by the Steam Packet Board on 30th October that the *Lady of Mann* would be retained for the 1996 season. The services of the SeaCat were dispensed with and the 'Lady' was to be employed to cover the *King Orry's* refit, the TT Races and a full summer of tourist traffic.

The *Lady of Mann* arrived back in the Mersey from Madeira on 16th November and berthed in Cammell Laird's wet basin at Birkenhead.

Meanwhile the decision not to operate a fast craft in 1996 caused uproar on the Isle of Man and an emergency three member select committee of Tynwald was set up to discuss the situation.

The *Lady of Mann* arrived in Douglas on 8th February 1996 and covered for the *King Orry* until 9th March. She demonstrated that she had lost none of her agility, even in her 21st year, when on 21st February she crossed from Heysham to Douglas, berth to berth, in 2 hours 53 minutes.

SEA CONTAINERS AT THE HELM

Shortly after 08.00 on Friday 29th March 1996 it was announced that the Isle of Man Steam Packet Company had lost its independence after 166 years of operation. Sea Containers now owned 58% of the shares in the Company. This whole issue had been simmering since the 1985 merger with Manx Line.

The 'Lady' commenced her 1996 summer season on Thursday 23rd May and went straight into the build-up of TT traffic. The almost predictable TT Week gale duly arrived on 31st May and the 'Lady' was running up to 4 hours late. The following day the electrics on

On 12th June 1995, the ***Lady of Mann*** completed her final crossing of the season from Douglas and is seen coming up the Mersey. *(J.R. Clague)*

Heysham's South Quay linkspan failed. It was low water and by the time repairs were effected the structure was partially submerged by the rising tide. This resulted in a backlog of five vessels waiting to use the linkspan, with the *King Orry* on her way over from Douglas to add to the queue. In the midst of this chaos the *Lady of Mann* was substituted on the Heysham service and once again the sideloader's amazing versatility was shown to the full as she as able to discharge and load at a quayside berth without requiring the linkspan.

The *Lady of Mann* met up with the USS *John F. Kennedy* on the Tynwald Fair Day excursion to Dublin on 5th July and had an uneventful summer's sailings. At the end of August 1996 it was announced that a new route between Fleetwood and Dublin would be tried out in October using the *Lady of Mann* with an estimated passage time of 6 hours 30 minutes. The 'Lady's' first sailing left Fleetwood on 26th September and carried just 175 passengers and 29 cars. The first 100 passengers had been given free tickets; there were some 30 media representatives and company officials on board, so there wasn't much of a payload! In a strong southerly gale the 'Lady' took 7 hours 15 minutes to reach Dublin. On Mondays a duty-free day-excursion to Dublin was offered at a £5 fare and on 30th September 780 passengers sailed from Fleetwood who were prepared to spend 14 hours at sea for the privilege of buying duty-free goods! Crossings between Fleetwood and Dublin operated on Thursdays, Fridays and Mondays throughout October and on Saturdays and Sundays day-excursions from Fleetwood to Douglas were on offer at £15. The final Fleetwood to Dublin sailing on Monday 28th October was delayed from 10.00 until 22.00 by severe southerly gales. Some 650 Irish visitors were attempting to return home after the Irish Bank Holiday weekend. After completing the crossings, the *Lady of Mann* laid up at Birkenhead.

The *Lady of Mann* covered the *King Orry's* 1997 overhaul period from 28th January until 17th February. In the spring it was announced that a fast craft would be in service again on Manx routes during the 1997 summer season, and that a new Liverpool and Dublin service would commence on 12th June, to be operated by the 'Lady.' The service would operate on a daily basis, but on Wednesdays the *SeaCat Isle of Man* would take over to allow the *Lady of Mann* to work the Fleetwood to Douglas day excursion sailing. The 'Lady' entered

With Captain Kinley acting as undocking pilot, the Madeira registered ***Lady of Mann*** leaves the Alfred Dock at Birkenhead for the Landing Stage on 17th July 1995. *(John Shepherd)*

Wright & Beyer's Bidston drydock in Birkenhead's West Float for her own overhaul on Tuesday 15th April

The *Lady of Mann* left Liverpool for Dublin on Sunday 18th May with 800 passengers. This was a positioning run for a film charter and for the next three days she featured in the making of Universal Studios' new film *'The Boxer'*. Leaving Dublin at 16.30 on Wednesday 21st May the 'Lady' was back in Liverpool just after 22.30.

1997 - LLANDUDNO AGAIN

The following morning the *Lady of Mann* left Liverpool at 07.00 on a positioning run to Llandudno Pier with 100 passengers on board. To celebrate the Pier's centenary a special Llandudno-Douglas day-excursion had been arranged, the first since 1982 when the *Manxman* operated the sailings. A full complement of passengers left Llandudno at 10.30 and arrived in Douglas at 13.30. The return sailing left the Isle of Man at 1830, called at Llandudno between 21.30 and 22.30, and just 70 passengers returned to Liverpool, arriving at 01.00 on the 23rd May.

Following the usual intensive pattern of TT Race Week sailings, the *Lady of Mann* opened the Liverpool - Dublin service on Thursday 12th June 1997, departing at 09.02 with 364 passengers and 84 cars.

The 'Lady's' arrival at Funchal on 21st July. *(Manuel Gouveia)*

She crossed to Dublin in 6 hours 30 minutes. Traffic levels on the new route built up rapidly and by mid-summer some 600 passengers and a capacity load of 130 cars were regularly being carried. With a favourable tide the crossing was often completed in less than six hours.

On Wednesday 6th August the *Lady of Mann* operated a Douglas to Fleetwood day-excursion and during her lay-over at Fleetwood sailed on a special three-hour cruise, passing close inshore at Blackpool and visiting the Morecambe Bay oil rigs. This unique cruise carried 250 passengers at a fare of £12.50 which included lunch. In bad weather on 3rd September the Fleetwood excursion was cancelled and the ship operated the Liverpool-Dublin service in place of the *SeaCat Isle of Man* which was stormbound

The *Lady of Mann* suffered a serious engine defect on Friday 7th November. She was about 1 hour 30 minutes from the Mersey Bar on the run from Dublin to Liverpool when the port crankshaft failed and she eventually berthed at Liverpool at 02.00 the following morning. The damage was far more serious than was first thought, and she did not return to service until 6th December. During this period she was drydocked and the underwater hull was painted a bright red, with no white-line division from the black hull. During her period off-service, intending passengers were transferred to the HSS *Stena Explorer* on the Holyhead-Dun Laoghaire route.

In the run up to Christmas 1997 the *Lady of Mann* offered Christmas Lunch duty-free cruises to Dublin at a £15 fare, which included a 'served at your seat' five-course meal. Severe weather over Christmas and the New Year disrupted sailings and the crossings were cancelled on 1st and 3rd January 1998. On 4th January the 'Lady' took 8 hours to reach Dublin and she closed the service in somewhat calmer conditions on 5th January, after which she sailed to Douglas to relieve the *King Orry*. The 'Orry's' overhaul was completed on 29th January after which the *Lady of Mann* retired to Birkenhead's Vittoria Dock.

In mid-February 1998 the Isle of Man Steam Packet Company announced that the 'Lady' would operate a full Easter programme of sailings. The *King Orry* could not be released from the Heysham route as she was required there to supplement the *Peveril's* freight sailings. In fact the *Lady of Mann* was stored up and a crew placed on standby in early March as there were fears that the new *SuperSeaCat Two* would not be able to open the Dublin service because of a shortage of engine spares. In the event the SuperSeaCat did cover the inaugural sailings on 12th March and it was not until 9th April when the *Lady of Mann*

Dressed overall at Funchal, the 'Lady' prepares to embark her first cars. *(Manuel Gouveia)*

There's no place like home ..... Going astern from the Edward Pier on Easter Saturday 1981.

undocked from Birkenhead.

The 'Lady' came straight to the rescue of the SuperSeaCat which was stormbound and had engine problems - this situation being typical of the entire year's programme. The *Lady of Mann* left Liverpool for Douglas at 20.00 (for 19.00) on 9th April, and as she was scheduled to proceed from Douglas to Dublin in the early hours of 10th April, she had on board 100 or so SuperSeaCat Dublin-bound passengers and 30 Dublin cars. She returned to dock after Easter, despite the ongoing problems with the new fast craft, and was painted in Sea Containers blue.

NEW LIVERY

The Steam Packet 'logo' was removed from the ship's bridge front, along with the red ribbon which had run the length of her boat deck since her 1989 refurbishment. It was rumoured that the 'Lady' would visit Weymouth after the TT for berthing trials with a view to possible use on Channel Islands routes which parent company Sea Containers were then interested in operating.

The *Lady of Mann* operated a Fleetwood-Douglas day trip on 27th May and on the following day carried a full complement on a Llandudno-Douglas excursion. The TT Race Week sailings passed off uneventfully and the ship left Douglas at 11.30 on 16th June for Liverpool. After discharging at the landing stage she entered Cammell Laird's wet basin and a large blue whale was painted on both sides of her superstructure. Some of her seating was also removed to create a dance floor. The 'Lady' was off to the Azores for three months on bareboat charter to Acorline and sailed from the Mersey on the evening of 17th June on the four day passage to the Islands.

Whilst the 'Lady' was in the Azores the new purpose-built ro-ro ferry *Ben-my-Chree* entered service amid a storm of protest about the perceived inadequacy of her passenger accommodation. Shortly afterwards the sad and untimely death of the 'Lady's' highly popular master, Captain Vernon Kinley, took place. To many of the ship's followers the names of Captain Kinley and the *Lady of Mann* were inseparable - throughout the years they had made a wonderful partnership and Vernon's enthusiasm for his ship was never more evident in his 'Foreword' to the first edition of this publication.

The *Lady of Mann* returned to Liverpool from her Azores charter on 24th September and was placed on standby to cover for the SuperSeaCat. She came to the rescue on 18th October when in the first 'end of season blow' the *Ben-my-Chree*, *SeaCat Danmark* and the *SuperSeaCat Two* were all stormbound. In the event the 'Lady' maintained a Liverpool and Douglas service with no problems, proving once again what a superb seaboat she was.

The 'Lady' arrives at Douglas in her new blue livery in June 1989. *(Miles Cowsill)*

Due to the new *Ben-my-Chree's* inability to use the landing stage at Liverpool, the *SuperSeaCat Two* was rostered to cover the winter weekend Liverpool and Douglas sailings until 5th January. Almost every weekend the *Lady of Mann* was brought out of dock to cover for the fast craft in bad weather. In October, November and December 1998 the SuperSeaCat cancelled over a third of its scheduled crossings due to wave heights in the Irish Sea exceeding three metres and the *Lady of Mann* proved again that conventional back-up was an absolute necessity.

On Tuesday 29th December 1998 the *Lady of Mann* was one of the very few vessels to venture out into the Irish Sea. All fast craft were stormbound around the coast and the 'Lady' sailed from Liverpool at 11.00 for Dublin, arriving some seven hours later. It was the intention that she would then sail to Douglas with the stranded passengers following the cancellation of the *Ben-my-Chree's* scheduled Dublin-Douglas sailing. Just as she was leaving Dublin, however, her port propeller became entangled with a 'Yokohama' type fender. This necessitated a dry-docking at Dublin on 2nd January and she then returned to Liverpool on her starboard engine only.

The New Year weekend SuperSeaCat crossings between Liverpool and Douglas were all cancelled because of bad weather. The *Lady of Mann*, which could have coped with the conditions, was under repair and so the company had to resort to desperate measures which included chartering a Manx Airlines plane to move foot passengers to Liverpool. The 'Lady' was back in service on 8th January 1999 and the SuperSeaCat stood down for her annual overhaul.

The *Lady of Mann* was retained on the Irish Sea for the 1999 summer season principally to act as back-up for the new *Ben-my-Chree* on peak days. The 'Ben' had received an adverse reception on her

Above: On 22nd May 1997, the 'Lady' was alongside at Llandudno Pier and *below:* leaving the resort astern with a helicopter escort and the Great Orme. *(both Captain Vernon Kinley)*

The ***Lady of Mann*** enjoys the heat of the Azores. She was chartered to run between five islands in summer 2000 and returned to the Mersey on 24th September. *(Bryan Kennedy)*

introduction in 1998 due to her limited passenger accommodation and the Company were restricting her passengers to 350 per crossing instead of the 500 she had a certificate to carry.

The *Lady of Mann* retained her tremendous enthusiast following, but the Isle of Man Steam Packet Company had perhaps been slow to appreciate and to capitalise on this. However, they must have been encouraged by the three Llandudno-Douglas day-excursions in 1999 which all carried a 900 passenger complement, and 600 were on board two Fleetwood-Douglas excursions.

On Saturday 24th July the *Lady of Mann* operated a special evening cruise to Port St Mary in memory of her popular master Captain Vernon Kinley who had died twelve months previously. In command for the cruise was Captain Kinley's old friend and colleague, Marine Superintendent Peter Corrin.

In June 1999 a Tynwald Select Committee on the Isle of Man Steam Packet Company published its report. The Committee had been set up following the introduction of the *Ben-my-Chree* and the inadequacy of the SuperSeaCats to cope with the Irish Sea in winter. The *Lady of Mann* received much favourable comment in the report and was praised as *'the best motor-cycle carrier in the fleet'* for the all important TT Race traffic.

The future of the 'Lady' was increasingly in doubt as 1999

The Steam Packet's ***Lady of Mann*** arriving at Warrenpoint on 16th June 2000. *(J.R. Clague)*

The 'Lady' at Workington on 15th June 2000. *(Jenny Williamson)*

progressed as she was reaching the point where SOLAS compliance would require heavy expenditure before the 2001 season. Recurring bad weather in the Irish Sea in the autumn and early winter of 1999 saw the ship deputising for the fast craft on 21 days.

The *Lady of Mann* covered the passenger sailings during the *Ben-my-Chree's* overhaul from 19th January until 7th February 2000. Following the usual hectic TT period she undertook a series of well-patrionised excursion sailings to the Isle of Man from Llandudno, Fleetwood, Whitehaven and Warrenpoint, culminating in a 'Round the Island' sailing on Saturday 17th June.

Following her successful charter to the Azores in the summer of 1998, Acorline repeated the venture in 2000. The *Lady of Mann* sailed for the islands on 25th June and was back in Liverpool on Sunday evening 24th September. Some Steam Packet engineering staff remained with her but otherwise she was locally crewed.

After two disappointing years of weather disruption to winter fast craft schedules, the decision was taken to place the *Lady of Mann* on the Liverpool and Douglas winter service from November 2000. This would lead to a more reliable service and would eliminate the expense of keeping her on stand-by in the event of bad weather cancellations by the fast craft. The *Lady of Mann* also covered the late October Irish Bank Holiday sailings due to more severe weather in the Irish Sea.

MAKEOVER AND FUTURE FOR THE 'LADY'

Although no official announcement had been forthcoming from the Company, it was evident that plans were well advanced for the upgrading of the *Lady of Mann* to meet SOLAS requirements. Without this upgrade the 'Lady' would be unable to operate after the expiration of her certificates on 23rd May 2001. Watertight doors were to be fitted on the main car deck and this would inevitably lead to some loss of capacity, and a slowing down in the rate of loading and discharge of vehicles.

The *Lady of Mann* completed her winter service on 26th February 2001 and entered Cammell Laird's wet basin for work to start on her overhaul and SOLAS upgrading. Apart from the fitting of three watertight bulkheads on the car deck, a new high speed rescue craft has been fitted on the starboard side, between the second and third lifeboats. In addition, new M.E.S. exit doors have been cut into the superstructure immediately below the bridge wings.

The devastating outbreak of foot and mouth disease on mainland U.K. in spring 2001 led to the decision on 24th April to cancel the TT Races in an effort to prevent the disease reaching the Isle of Man. The *Lady of Mann's* schedule was immediately cancelled, including the Whitehaven, Llandudno and Fleetwood excursions. A special 25th anniversary sailing to the 'Lady's' birthplace at Troon was sadly also abandoned.

The *Lady of Mann* left Cammell Laird's wet basin on 11th June.

The 'Lady' and the ***Ben-my-Chree*** at Heysham during their 2000 season. This view shows the 'Ben' swinging off her berth inward from Douglas. *(Jenny Williamson)*

The ‘Lady’ and the ***SuperSeaCat Two*** at the port of Heysham on 5th June 2000. The fast craft is underway for Belfast. *(Jenny Williamson)*

She will almost certainly never return there following the spectacular *Costa Classica* fiasco which led to the closure of the yard. She sailed for Douglas where she was open for public inspection and on 15th June sailed for the Azores and a three month charter.

Following a successful summer, the *Lady of Mann* was back in Liverpool on 24th September. She has covered for bad weather cancellations before operating the Liverpool and Douglas winter service and the Heysham-Douglas passenger sailings during the *Ben-my-Chree's* overhaul in January and February 2002.

The future of the *Lady of Mann* would appear to be secure for the next five, or hopefully ten, years. The Isle of Man Steam Packet Company has recognised that the sturdy *Lady of Mann* can operate a reliable and comfortable service in all but the very worst conditions. The ship is a superb sea boat built with the experience and knowledge gained from operating in the Irish Sea from 1830-1976. There is no doubt that the *Lady of Mann* is by far and away the best motorcycle carrier for the annual TT Race traffic and her summer charters to the Azores provide useful revenue when she is not needed on the Irish Sea.

The *Lady of Mann* has a loyal and enthusiastic band of followers, just as the preserved paddle steamer *Waverley* has. Hopefully this can be exploited in the form of a more extensive and imaginative programme of excursion sailings in the late spring before the arrival of the TT traffic. Whilst appreciating that these excursions have to

Part of the refurbished forward lounge following the 2001 refit. *(IOMSPC)*

A view of the refurbished Cafe Express area introduced on board the ***Lady of Mann*** in 2001. *(IOMSPC)*

The ***Lady of Mann*** leaves Douglas on her 'Round the Island' sailing on Saturday 17th June 2000. *(Miles Cowsill)*

The 'Lady' gets underway from Douglas for Liverpool at the end of her busy TT season. *(Miles Cowsill)*

operate at an acceptably low fare, and that there is no revenue from vehicles, it would seem in the light of experience there is scope for extension.

SURVIVOR

Few of us who stood on the King Edward Pier at Douglas on that fine sunny evening of 28th June 1976 and watched the new *Lady of Mann* arrive from her builders could have had any idea of just how passenger shipping operations to the Isle of Man would change over the next 25 years. The *Lady of Mann* joined a seven ship fleet which still contained three classic steam turbines. The 'Lady' has survived the turbulent years of Manx Line, the 1985 merger, the 1996 take-over and has had her own future placed in doubt on numerous occasions. The one great constant in all the stream of problems, setbacks and fiascos of the last quarter century has been the *Lady of Mann*.

The *Lady of Mann* is a survivor and hopefully she will survive for another ten years.

Dedicated to the memory of Captain Vernon Kinley
of the Isle of Man Steam Packet Company Ltd.,
late Master of the motor vessel *Lady of Mann*.

LADY OF MANN - SPECIFICATIONS:

Builder:	Ailsa Shipbuilding Company Limited, Troon, Ayrshire (Yard No 547)
Engines:	Two 12 Cylinder Pielstick Diesels, developing 11,500 bhp. Built by Crossley Premier Engines, Manchester
Official No:	359761
Call Sign:	G V E Q
Tonnage:	As built in 1976: Gross 2,990, Nett 1,326, Deadweight 500. After 1989 rebuild: Gross 3,176, Nett 1,467, Deadweight 770
Length:	104.43 metres overall, 98.15 metres between perpendiculars
Breadth:	16.74 metres extreme, 15.85 metres moulded
Draft:	3.633 metres
Speed:	18 knots service, 23 knots maximum
Passengers:	1,600 from entry into service until 1988 1,200 in 1988 1,000 following completion of 1989 rebuild 800/656/460 following 2001 building works

The ***Lady of Mann*** leaves the Landing Stage at Liverpool following her major overhaul in 2001. *(IOMSPC)*

Cars/Vans:	approximately 100 from 1976 until 1988 approximately 130 following 1989 rebuild approximately 115 following 2001 rebuild
Clear Height:	2.20 metres
Fuel Bunkers:	162.5 tonnes capacity

ACKNOWLEDGEMENTS

The author and publishers would like to thank the following people for their assistance with '*Lady of Mann* - Last of the Line': Malcolm McRonald, Jenny and John Williamson, Bryan Kennedy, Manuel Gouveia, Dick Clague, Rob Fleming, Pat Somner of Ferry Publications and particularly Hamish Ross, Managing Dirctor of the Isle of Man Steam Packet Co. Ltd. for agreeing to write the Foreword.

Editor: John Hendy *Design*: Miles Cowsill